The 21st Century Leader

Karngong Lovett Tangwa

Published by Sparker Africa

Abuja - Nigeria

ISBN: 979-8-8787-8777-2

Disclaimer

DEDICATION

To God, You are the source of all wisdom, creativity, and inspiration. As I pen these words and embark on this journey, I dedicate this book to You, the ultimate author of life. Your boundless love and grace have been my guiding light, illuminating my path in moments of darkness and uncertainty. Your unwavering presence has instilled in me the strength to overcome challenges and embrace the opportunities that lie ahead.

In Your infinite wisdom, You have bestowed upon me the gift of expression, allowing me to share my thoughts and ideas with the world. I humbly offer this book as a testament to Your divine grace, knowing that every word written is a reflection of Your wisdom. May the pages within these covers be a vessel for Your truth and an instrument for positive change in the lives of others. May Your light shine through these words, touching hearts, and inspiring minds.

With gratitude and humility, I place this work into Your hands, trusting that You will use it for Your divine purpose. May it be a small offering of gratitude for the immeasurable blessings You have bestowed upon me.

I dedicate this book to You, the Creator and Sustainer of all things, with the hope that it may bring honor and glory to Your name.

In awe of Your greatness.

About the "The 21st Century Leader"

This comprehensive book explores the essential aspects of leadership in the context of the rapidly evolving 21st century. It delves into topics such as adapting to technological advancements, harnessing the potential of smart kids, and navigating the changing landscape of leadership.

Throughout the book, we have examined the qualities, skills, and mindset required to be an effective leader in the 21st century. We have explored various leadership styles, communication strategies, and methods for inspiring and motivating teams. Moreover, we have emphasized the importance of continuous learning, adaptability, and embracing diversity and inclusion in leadership.

Drawing inspiration from real-life leaders, successful entrepreneurs, and influential figures from diverse fields, we have highlighted the lessons and principles that can guide aspiring and current leaders on their journey towards excellence.

"The 21st Century Leader" serves as a roadmap for navigating the challenges and opportunities of leadership in the modern era. It encourages leaders to be adaptable, forward-thinking, and ethical in their approach, while also emphasizing the significance of personal well-being, self-care, and building meaningful connections.

Table of Contents

Acknowledgment

I am profoundly grateful to the following individuals who have played pivotal roles in shaping my journey as a leader and as a person. Their wisdom, inspiration, and unwavering support have been instrumental in my growth and development:

Apostle Joshua Selman: Your teachings on positive leadership and unwavering commitment to spiritual and personal growth have been a guiding light in my life. Your ability to connect with hearts and minds and inspire transformative change is truly remarkable. I am deeply grateful for the profound impact you have had on my leadership journey.

John C. Maxwell: Your inspiring leadership lessons and timeless principles have been a constant source of motivation for me. Your books and teachings have provided invaluable insights into effective leadership and personal development. I am honored to have learned from your wisdom and experience.

Pastor Skambo Morrison: Your inspirational teachings and unwavering faith have been a source of strength and hope during challenging times. Your guidance and mentorship have helped me navigate through obstacles and keep my vision alive. I am forever thankful for your presence in my life.

To each of you, I extend my deepest appreciation for your selflessness, dedication, and willingness to impart knowledge and wisdom to others. Your impact goes beyond words, and I am blessed to have had the opportunity to learn from each of you.

I also want to acknowledge the numerous friends, mentors, and family members who have supported and encouraged me throughout this journey. Your belief in me and your encouragement have been instrumental in my growth, and I am truly grateful for your presence in my life.

Lastly, I would like to express my heartfelt gratitude to all the readers and followers who have embraced my work and allowed me the privilege of leading. Your engagement and feedback have been invaluable, and I am humbled by your support.

With profound gratitude,

Karngong Lovett Tangwa

Chapter One

THE CHANGING LANDSCAPE OF LEADERSHIP IN THE 21ST CENTURY

Introduction

Welcome to the world of leadership in the 21st century—a landscape that is constantly evolving, driven by the rapid advancement of technology, the rise of smart kids, and the ever-increasing pace of change. As a leader in this era, you are faced with unique challenges and opportunities that demand a new set of skills and approaches. In this introductory chapter, we will explore the profound impact of these changes and set the stage for understanding the essence of 21st-century leadership.

The Impact of Technology

Technology has revolutionized every aspect of our lives, and its influence on leadership is undeniable. The advent of the internet, artificial intelligence, automation, and other technological advancements has disrupted traditional business models, transformed industries, and changed the way we work and communicate. As a leader, you must not only keep up with these changes but also harness technology to drive innovation, productivity, and collaboration within your organization.

One of the key impacts of technology is the increased interconnectedness and globalization of the world. Geographic boundaries are no longer barriers to communication and collaboration. Virtual teams have become the norm, requiring leaders to navigate the complexities of leading remote employees and fostering a sense of belonging and engagement despite physical distance.

Moreover, technology has empowered individuals with access to vast amounts of information, enabling them to be more informed, critical thinkers. This phenomenon, often referred to as the "information age," has given rise to smart kids—individuals who are digitally savvy, well-informed, and eager to contribute their ideas and insights. As a leader, it is essential to recognize and leverage the potential of these smart kids, creating an environment that encourages their growth and empowers them to make a positive impact.

Embracing Change

The 21st century is characterized by rapid and continuous change. As a leader, you must not only adapt to change but also foster a culture that embraces it. Change can be disruptive and uncomfortable, but it also presents opportunities for growth and innovation. *Leaders who resist change risk being left behind,* while those who embrace it can seize new possibilities and drive their organizations forward.

Embracing change requires a mindset shift—a willingness to challenge the status quo, explore new ideas, and experiment with different approaches. It also involves cultivating resilience and agility to navigate the uncertainties and complexities that accompany change. As a leader, you must be open to learning, unlearning, and relearning, constantly seeking new knowledge and staying attuned to emerging trends and technologies.

The Essence of 21st-Century Leadership:
In this rapidly changing landscape, what defines an effective leader in the 21st century? While the core principles of leadership remain timeless—such as integrity, vision, and empathy—the context in which leaders operate has evolved. The following key traits are essential for success in the 21st century:

1. **Adaptability:** As mentioned earlier, adaptability is crucial in a world of constant change. A 21st-century leader must be flexible, agile, and open-minded, able to pivot strategies and approaches as circumstances evolve.

2. **Emotional Intelligence:** In a digitally connected yet emotionally disconnected world, emotional intelligence is more critical than ever. Leaders must possess empathy, self-awareness, and the ability to connect with and inspire their team members on a deeper level.

3. **Technological Fluency:** Leaders need not be technology experts, but they must possess a solid understanding of the technological landscape. This fluency enables them to make informed decisions, leverage technology effectively, and communicate with their tech-savvy teams. Technology has become an integral part of our daily lives. Its influence extends beyond industries and

businesses; it has also revolutionized the way we communicate, learn, and worship. As a leader, it is crucial to be technologically fluent and embrace the advancements that shape the landscape of leadership in the 21st century.

4. Visionary Thinking: Crafting a compelling vision and communicating it effectively is paramount. A visionary leader inspires others, provides direction, and creates a sense of purpose and meaning.

5. Collaboration and Inclusivity: In a diverse and interconnected world, collaboration and inclusivity are critical. 21st-century leaders must foster an environment where diverse perspectives are valued, ideas are shared openly, and teamwork is encouraged.

6. Continuous Learning: Learning is a lifelong journey, especially in the rapidly changing landscape of the 21st century. Leaders must embrace a growth mindset, actively seek new knowledge, and encourage a culture of continuous learning within their organizations.

7. Ethical Leadership: Ethical considerations are paramount in the digital age. Leaders must navigate complex ethical dilemmas, promote integrity and transparency, and build a culture of ethical conduct within their organizations.

As we embark on this exploration of leadership in the 21st century, it is crucial to recognize the significant impact of technology, the rise of smart kids, and the ever-present need to embrace change. By cultivating the key traits of adaptability, emotional intelligence, technological fluency, visionary thinking, collaboration and inclusivity, continuous learning, and ethical leadership, you will be equipped to navigate the challenges and seize the opportunities of this dynamic era.

Throughout this book, we will delve deeper into each of these traits, providing practical insights, real-life examples, and actionable strategies to help you develop and enhance your leadership skills. By embracing the essence of 21st-century leadership, you can become an effective leader who not only navigates the complexities of the digital age but also inspires and empowers others to thrive in this ever-evolving world.

In the following chapters, we will explore each aspect of 21st-century leadership in greater detail, providing you with the tools and knowledge to become a successful leader in the midst of technological advancements, the rise of smart kids, and the continuous changes that define the 21st century. So, let's embark on this transformative journey together and unlock your full leadership potential in the 21st century.

Chapter Two

THE FUNDAMENTAL NATURE OF LEADERSHIP IN THE 21ST CENTURY

The Fundamental Nature of Leadership in the 21st Century

In this era of technological advancements, interconnected economies, and diverse societies, effective leadership requires a unique set of skills, qualities, and perspectives. Now, let's delve deeper into the essence of leadership itself. What does it mean to be a leader in the 21st century? What are the core qualities and principles that guide exceptional leaders in this rapidly evolving world? In this chapter, we will explore these questions and provide insights into the fundamental elements of leadership in the 21st century.

The Foundation of Leadership

Leadership is not solely about occupying a position of authority or power. It is about inspiring and influencing others to achieve a common purpose or vision. *At its core, leadership is based on trust, integrity, and the ability to create positive change.* Whether you lead a small team, a large organization, or a community initiative, the essence of leadership remains consistent.

Adaptive and Transformational Leadership

Given the ever-changing landscape of the 21st century, leaders must be adaptable and willing to embrace change. Adaptive leadership involves the ability to navigate uncertainty, learn from failures, and adjust strategies in response to evolving circumstances. Transformational leadership, on the other hand, focuses on inspiring and empowering others to reach their full potential. By setting a compelling vision, fostering innovation, and encouraging growth, transformational leaders create a positive impact on their teams and organizations.

Integrity and Ethics

In the age of technology and digital connectivity, maintaining integrity and ethical conduct is paramount for leaders. Trust is the foundation of effective leadership, and leaders must demonstrate honesty, transparency, and a strong ethical compass. By consistently upholding ethical standards and making principled decisions, leaders inspire trust, loyalty, and commitment from their team members.

Courage and Resilience

Leadership in the 21st century requires courage and resilience. It takes courage to take calculated risks, challenge the status quo, and pursue ambitious goals. Leaders must also possess the resilience to bounce back from setbacks, learn from failures, and adapt to adversity. By modeling courage and resilience, leaders inspire their teams to persevere in the face of challenges and embrace a growth mindset.

Servant Leadership

Servant leadership is a powerful approach that emphasizes the leader's commitment to serving the needs of others. In the 21st century, where collaboration and empowerment are essential, servant leaders prioritize the growth and well-being of their team members. They provide support, guidance, and resources, and actively seek opportunities to help others succeed. By fostering a culture of servant leadership, leaders create an environment of trust, collaboration, and shared success.

Emotional Intelligence

In the 21st century, emotional intelligence is a crucial attribute for effective leaders. Emotional intelligence encompasses self-awareness, empathy, social skills, and self-regulation. Leaders who possess high emotional intelligence are adept at understanding and managing their own emotions while being attuned to the emotions and needs of others. This enables them to build strong relationships, inspire trust, and navigate complex interpersonal dynamics. We will delve deeper into emotional intelligence in the next chapter.

In the following chapters, we will explore practical strategies and tools to develop these core qualities and principles of leadership. We will examine how to enhance emotional intelligence, foster adaptability, lead with integrity, embrace courage and resilience, and cultivate a servant leadership mindset by incorporating these elements.

Chapter Three

EMOTIONAL INTELLIGENCE IN LEADERSHIP

Emotional Intelligence in Leadership

Emotional intelligence plays a pivotal role in effective leadership, enabling leaders to understand, connect with, and inspire their team members on a deeper level. In this chapter, we will delve into the concept of emotional intelligence and its significance in leadership.

Understanding Emotional Intelligence

Emotional intelligence refers to the ability to recognize, understand, and manage one's own emotions, as well as to perceive and respond to the emotions of others. It involves self-awareness, self-regulation, empathy, and effective interpersonal skills. Emotional intelligence allows leaders to build strong relationships, navigate conflicts, inspire trust, and foster a positive work environment.

Daniel Goleman, renowned psychologist and author, encapsulates the importance of emotional intelligence in leadership in his book "Primal Leadership: Unleashing the Power of Emotional Intelligence".

"Effective leadership is not about making speeches or being liked; leadership is defined by results, not attributes." - Daniel Goleman

Goleman emphasizes that leadership effectiveness goes beyond surface-level attributes. It is rooted in the ability to understand and manage emotions, both in oneself and in others, to drive meaningful results.

Chimamanda Ngozi Adichie, a Nigerian author and activist, demonstrates the power of empathy in her storytelling. Through her novels, she creates deeply relatable characters and explores complex human emotions. Adichie's ability to connect with readers on an emotional level fosters understanding, empathy, and a sense of shared humanity. Her work exemplifies how emotional intelligence can be channeled through art to create meaningful impact.

Joseph, from the biblical story of Joseph and his brothers, exhibited remarkable emotional intelligence. Despite enduring betrayal and adversity, Joseph managed his emotions and demonstrated empathy towards his brothers when they sought his help during a famine. He displayed forgiveness, compassion, and understanding, showcasing emotional intelligence in his leadership role.

The Components of Emotional Intelligence

1. Self-Awareness: Self-awareness is the foundation of emotional intelligence. It involves recognizing and understanding one's own emotions, strengths, weaknesses, values, and impact on others. Leaders who possess self-awareness are better able to manage their emotions, make sound decisions, and communicate authentically. By understanding their own emotional triggers and biases, they can navigate challenging situations with composure and empathy.

"Knowing yourself is the beginning of all wisdom." - Aristotle

Aristotle's quote emphasizes the importance of self-awareness as the starting point for personal growth and leadership wisdom. Leaders who possess self-awareness are more equipped to understand and lead themselves effectively.

2. Empathy: Empathy is the ability to understand and share the feelings of others. In a leadership context, empathy allows leaders to connect with their team members, recognize their needs and concerns, and provide support and guidance. Leaders who demonstrate empathy create an inclusive and supportive work environment where individuals feel valued and understood.

"Empathy is about finding echoes of another person in yourself." - Mohsin Hamid

Mohsin Hamid's quote from one of his books, "How to get filthy rich in rising Asia" beautifully captures the essence of empathy. It highlights the ability to relate to others, to see their perspectives, and to recognize our shared human experiences. Leaders who practice empathy create a sense of belonging and foster a collaborative and compassionate culture.

3. Effective Communication: Emotional intelligence enhances communication skills, enabling leaders to express themselves clearly, listen actively, and adapt their communication style to different individuals and situations. Leaders who communicate effectively build trust, resolve conflicts, and inspire their teams to achieve common goals.

In the book "Management: Tasks, Responsibilities, Practices" by peter Drucker, he said;

"The most important thing in communication is hearing what isn't said." - Peter Drucker

Leaders who possess emotional intelligence are attuned to the unspoken messages and emotions beneath the surface, allowing them to foster meaningful connections and build stronger relationships.

3. Self-Regulation: Self-regulation refers to the ability to manage and control one's emotions and impulses. Leaders who possess self-regulation are adept at maintaining composure, managing stress, and making rational decisions even in challenging situations. They exhibit self-discipline and are able to adapt their behavior to align with their values and long-term goals.

"Emotional self-control is the essence of leadership." - Daniel Goleman

Daniel Goleman's quote emphasizes that emotional self-control lies at the heart of effective leadership. Leaders who can regulate their emotions are better equipped to navigate conflicts, make thoughtful decisions, and lead with calmness and clarity.

4. Interpersonal/Social Skills: Interpersonal skills are vital for building strong relationships, fostering collaboration, and influencing others. Leaders with strong interpersonal skills possess effective communication, conflict resolution, and empathy. They are skilled at understanding and responding to the needs and perspectives of others, creating a positive and productive work environment.

"Effective leaders are made not born. They learn from trying and failing, and they have the patience to learn and develop over time." - Marshall Goldsmith

Marshall Goldsmith's quote emphasizes the importance of interpersonal skills as learnable qualities. Leadership is not an innate talent but a skill that can be developed through practice, feedback, and continuous learning. By honing their interpersonal skills, leaders can foster meaningful connections and inspire their teams to reach new heights.

In this chapter, we have explored the significance of emotional intelligence in leadership. We have seen how emotional intelligence encompasses self-awareness, empathy, effective communication, self-regulation, and interpersonal skills. By developing and nurturing these aspects of emotional intelligence, leaders can enhance their ability to connect with others, make sound decisions, and create a positive and motivating work environment.

As we move forward in this book, we will delve into practical strategies for developing emotional intelligence, including self-reflection exercises, communication techniques, and tools for managing emotions and stress. By actively engaging in these strategies, you will strengthen your emotional intelligence and become a more effective leader in the 21st century.

In the upcoming chapters, we will continue our exploration of essential leadership qualities and delve deeper into topics such as adaptability, integrity, resilience, and servant leadership. Together, we will unlock the full potential of your leadership capabilities and navigate the challenges and opportunities of the 21st century.

Chapter Four

ADAPTABILITY AND RESILIENCE IN LEADERSHIP

Adaptability and Resilience in Leadership

As a leader in the 21st century, you must possess the qualities of adaptability and resilience. These attributes enable leaders to navigate uncertainty, embrace change, and inspire their teams to overcome challenges and seize opportunities. In this chapter, we will explore the importance of adaptability and resilience in leadership and provide insights from renowned authors, along with real-life and fictional stories that exemplify these qualities.

The Power of Adaptability

Adaptability is the ability to adjust and thrive in the face of changing circumstances. It involves embracing new ideas, approaches, and technologies, and being open to different perspectives. Leaders who are adaptable demonstrate flexibility, creativity, and a willingness to learn and grow.

"Adaptability is about the powerful difference between adapting to cope and adapting to win." - Max McKeown

Max McKeown, in his book "Adaptability: The Art of Winning in an Age of Uncertainty," emphasizes that adaptability is not merely about surviving but about thriving in the face of uncertainty. Leaders who embrace adaptability not only navigate change effectively but also seize opportunities for growth and success.

Satya Nadella, the CEO of Microsoft, exemplifies adaptability in leadership. When he took the helm in 2014, Microsoft was facing challenges in a rapidly evolving tech industry. Nadella recognized the need for a shift in mindset and strategy. He transformed Microsoft from a predominantly desktop-oriented company to a cloud-first, mobile-focused organization. Under his leadership, Microsoft embraced new technologies, fostered collaboration, and repositioned itself as a leader in the industry. Nadella's adaptability propelled Microsoft's resurgence and positioned it for future success.

The Strength of Resilience

Resilience is the ability to bounce back from setbacks, overcome obstacles, and persevere in the face of adversity. It involves maintaining a positive mindset, learning from failures, and adapting to change with resilience.

"Resilience is accepting your new reality, even if it's less good than the one you had before." - Elizabeth Edwards

Elizabeth Edwards, in her book "Resilience: Reflections on the Burdens and Gifts of Facing Life's Adversities," highlights the importance of accepting and adapting to new realities. Resilient leaders acknowledge setbacks and challenges but maintain the determination and courage to move forward and create positive change.

In J.K. Rowling's popular "Harry Potter" series, the character of Harry Potter demonstrates resilience in the face of numerous trials and tribulations. From battling dark forces to enduring personal losses, Harry continually rises above adversity. He learns from setbacks, draws strength from his support network, and remains committed to his purpose. Harry's resilience enables him to face challenges head-on and emerge stronger, ultimately triumphing over the darkest of circumstances.

Nelson Mandela, the iconic South African leader and anti-apartheid activist, exemplifies resilience in leadership. Throughout his life, Mandela faced immense challenges, including imprisonment for 27 years. Despite the hardships, he never wavered in his commitment to justice, equality, and the dismantling of apartheid. Mandela's resilience, unwavering resolve, and ability to forgive and reconcile were instrumental in South Africa's transition to democracy.

Adaptability and resilience are indispensable qualities for leaders in the 21st century. Leaders who are adaptable embrace change, seize opportunities, and foster innovation. Resilient leaders bounce back from setbacks, maintain a positive mindset, and persevere in the face of challenges.

Chapter Five

INTEGRITY AND ETHICS IN LEADERSHIP

Integrity and Ethics in Leadership

Integrity and ethics are fundamental pillars of effective leadership in the 21st century. Leaders who demonstrate unwavering integrity and ethical conduct inspire trust, build strong relationships, and foster a culture of accountability. In this chapter, we will explore the importance of integrity and ethics in leadership, examining their impact on organizational success and personal credibility.

The Essence of Integrity

Integrity is the alignment of one's actions and values, displaying honesty, transparency, and consistency. Leaders with integrity demonstrate ethical behavior, take responsibility for their actions, and uphold moral principles even in challenging circumstances. They inspire trust and credibility among their team members and stakeholders.

"Real integrity is doing the right thing, knowing that nobody's going to know whether you did it or not." - Oprah Winfrey

Oprah Winfrey's quote encapsulates the essence of integrity. True integrity lies in doing what is right, even when no one is watching or there is no external reward or recognition. Leaders who prioritize integrity are guided by their inner compass and hold themselves accountable to the highest standards of ethical conduct.

Ethical Decision-Making

Ethical decision-making involves considering the moral implications of actions and choices, and prioritizing fairness, honesty, and the greater good. Ethical leaders engage in thoughtful reflection, seek diverse perspectives, and make choices aligned with their values and ethical principles.

"The ultimate measure of a man is not where he stands in moments of comfort and convenience, but where he stands at times of challenge and controversy." - Martin Luther King Jr.

Martin Luther King Jr.'s quote emphasizes the importance of ethical decision-making in times of challenge and controversy. Ethical leaders demonstrate their true character and values when faced with difficult choices, staying true to their principles and making decisions that align with their moral compass.

Patagonia, the outdoor clothing and gear company, is known for its commitment to environmental stewardship and ethical practices. The company's founder, Yvon Chouinard, prioritized environmental sustainability and ethical manufacturing practices long before it became a popular trend. Patagonia actively works towards reducing its ecological footprint, supports environmental causes, and transparently communicates its efforts. The company's commitment to integrity and ethics has not only earned it a loyal customer base but has also set an example for responsible business practices.

The Power of Ethical Leadership

Ethical leaders create a culture of trust, fairness, and accountability within their organizations. They lead by example, promoting ethical conduct, and ensuring that policies and practices align with ethical standards. Ethical leaders inspire their teams to uphold high moral principles, fostering a positive work environment and sustainable long-term success.

"Failing organizations are usually over-managed and under-led." - Warren Bennis

Warren Bennis's quote highlights the distinction between management and leadership. Ethical leadership goes beyond managing processes and tasks; it involves setting a clear ethical direction and leading by example. Leaders who prioritize ethics guide their organizations towards long-term success and sustainable growth.

Integrity and ethics are foundational qualities of effective leadership in the 21st century. Leaders who prioritize integrity demonstrate ethical behavior, inspire trust, and build strong relationships. Ethical decision-making ensures that leaders act in alignment with their values and make choices that consider the greater good. By embodying integrity and ethical conduct, leaders create a culture of trust, accountability, and ethical excellence.

Chapter Six

COURAGEOUS LEADERSHIP IN THE FACE OF ADVERSITY

Courageous Leadership in the Face of Adversity

Courageous leadership is a vital attribute for navigating the challenges and uncertainties of the 21st century. Leaders who display courage inspire their teams to persevere, take bold actions, and embrace innovation. In this chapter, we will explore the importance of courage in leadership, examining how it drives positive change and fosters resilience. We will also include insightful quotes from renowned authors and real-life stories of leaders who exemplify courageous leadership.

The Nature of Courage

Courage is the ability to face fear, uncertainty, and adversity with determination and resolve. Courageous leaders are willing to take calculated risks, challenge the status quo, and stand up for what they believe is right. They lead with conviction, even when the path ahead is uncertain, and inspire their teams to push beyond their comfort zones.

"Courage is not the absence of fear, but rather the assessment that something else is more important than fear." - Franklin D. Roosevelt

Franklin D. Roosevelt's quote encapsulates the essence of courage. Courageous leaders acknowledge fear and uncertainty but prioritize a greater purpose or mission over their own apprehensions. Their commitment to a higher cause propels them forward, motivating their teams to face challenges with determination and resolve.

Malala Yousafzai, a Pakistani activist for female education and the youngest Nobel Prize laureate, epitomizes courageous leadership. Despite facing threats and violence from the Taliban for advocating girls' education, Malala remained steadfast in her commitment to promoting education and gender equality. In 2012, she survived a targeted assassination attempt, which only strengthened her resolve to continue her fight. Malala's courageous leadership has brought global attention to the importance of education for all, especially for girls in regions affected by conflict and inequality.

The Courage to Innovate

Innovation often requires taking risks and challenging the status quo. Courageous leaders encourage creativity and experimentation, knowing that breakthroughs arise from pushing boundaries and embracing failure as part of the learning process. They inspire a culture of innovation where individuals feel empowered to bring forth new ideas and solutions.

"Do not fear failure but rather fear not trying." - Roy T. Bennett

Roy T. Bennett's quote underscores the importance of overcoming the fear of failure. Courageous leaders recognize that failure is an inherent part of the journey to success and encourage their teams to embrace failure as a stepping stone towards growth and innovation.

Elon Musk, the visionary entrepreneur and CEO of SpaceX and Tesla, is an example of fictional leadership. Through his ambitious ventures, including the goal of colonizing Mars and accelerating the world's transition to sustainable energy, Musk has demonstrated unwavering courage. Despite facing numerous obstacles, financial challenges, and skepticism from critics, he remains resolute in pursuing his vision for a better future. Musk's courageous leadership has revolutionized the space exploration and electric vehicle industries, inspiring countless innovators and entrepreneurs.

Leading with Ethical Courage

Courageous leadership extends beyond taking risks and driving innovation; it also involves standing up for ethical principles, even when it means confronting difficult decisions or going against popular opinion. Leaders with ethical courage prioritize doing what is right over what is easy or expedient, even if it entails personal sacrifice.

"It takes a great deal of bravery to stand up to our enemies, but just as much to stand up to our friends." - J.K. Rowling, Harry Potter and the Sorcerer's Stone

J.K. Rowling's quote, spoken by Albus Dumbledore in the "Harry Potter" series, emphasizes the need for ethical courage in leadership. Leaders must have the courage to stand up for their values and principles, even when it means challenging those who may be considered friends or allies. Ethical courage requires a steadfast commitment to upholding what is right and just, even in the face of opposition.

Edith Cavell, a British nurse during World War I, exemplifies courageous leadership in the pursuit of ethical principles. Despite the risks involved, she assisted in the escape of Allied soldiers from German-occupied Belgium. Cavell believed in the duty to help those in need, regardless of nationality. Her actions were discovered, and she was arrested and sentenced to death. Even in the face of imminent execution, Cavell displayed unwavering courage, stating, **"Patriotism is not enough**". I must have no hatred or bitterness towards anyone." Her bravery and commitment to her ethical principles continue to inspire leaders around the world.

Courageous leadership is essential in the 21st century, where change, uncertainty, and adversity are constant companions. Leaders who demonstrate courage inspire their teams to push boundaries, embrace innovation, and persevere in the face of challenges. They lead with conviction, prioritize ethical principles, and stand up for what is right. By embodying courageous leadership, individuals can drive positive change and create a better future for themselves, their organizations, and society as a whole.

Chapter Seven

SERVANT LEADERSHIP: LEADING WITH COMPASSION AND EMPATHY

Servant Leadership: Leading with Compassion and Empathy

Servant leadership is a powerful approach to leadership that focuses on serving others rather than seeking personal gain. In the 21st century, where empathy and compassion are vital, servant leadership has gained prominence as an effective leadership style. In this chapter, we will explore the concept of servant leadership, its impact on organizational success, and its relevance in the African context.

The Essence of Servant Leadership

Servant leadership is rooted in the idea that leaders should prioritize the needs of their team members and the community they serve. It involves actively listening, supporting, and empowering others to reach their full potential. Servant leaders lead with humility, empathy, and a genuine desire to make a positive difference.

"True leadership must be for the benefit of the followers, not to enrich the leader." - John C. Maxwell

John C. Maxwell's captures the essence of servant leadership. Leaders who prioritize the well-being and growth of their followers create an environment that fosters trust, collaboration, and personal development.

Dr. Ameyo Stella Adadevoh, a Nigerian physician, demonstrated exemplary servant leadership during the

2014 Ebola outbreak in Nigeria. As the Chief Consultant Physician at First Consultant Hospital in Lagos, she recognized the first case of Ebola in the country and took immediate action to isolate and treat the patient. Despite immense pressure and limited resources, Dr. Adadevoh prioritized the health and safety of her team, the patient, and the wider community. Tragically, she contracted the virus and lost her life. Her selfless sacrifice saved countless lives and exemplified the essence of servant leadership in the face of a public health crisis.

The life and teachings of Jesus Christ offer a profound example of servant leadership. Jesus consistently demonstrated humility, compassion, and selflessness in His interactions with His disciples and the wider community. He washed the feet of His disciples, showing that true leadership involves serving others and meeting their needs. Jesus prioritized healing, forgiveness, and empowerment, and He modeled a servant's heart, setting a powerful example for leaders in all spheres of life.

The Impact of Servant Leadership

Servant leadership creates a culture of trust, collaboration, and shared responsibility within organizations. By placing the needs of their team members first, servant leaders cultivate a sense of belonging and purpose, resulting in increased engagement, productivity, and overall well-being. This leadership style fosters loyalty and commitment among teams, contributing to long-term organizational success.

Mo Ibrahim, a Sudanese-British entrepreneur and philanthropist, exemplifies servant leadership through his commitment to the development of Africa. After establishing a successful telecommunications company, he dedicated his resources and influence to promoting good governance and leadership on the continent. The Mo Ibrahim Foundation awards the Ibrahim Prize for Achievement in African Leadership, recognizing exceptional African leaders who have demonstrated accountable and transparent governance. Ibrahim's philanthropic leadership embodies the principles of servant leadership, as he actively works towards empowering African leaders and driving positive change.

Servant leadership is a powerful approach to leadership that emphasizes compassion, empathy, and a genuine commitment to serving others. African leaders have the opportunity to embrace this leadership philosophy and make a lasting impact on their communities and organizations. By prioritizing the needs of their team members and cultivating a culture of servant leadership, individuals can create positive change, foster collaboration.

Chapter Eight

EFFECTIVE COMMUNICATION: THE KEY TO INSPIRING AND INFLUENCING OTHERS

Effective Communication: The Key to Inspiring and Influencing Others

Growing up as a young boy, when I heard the word communication what came to mind was just two people conversing, I never knew communication goes beyond just talking. Effective communication is more crucial than ever for leaders. The ability to articulate ideas, inspire others, and build meaningful connections is essential for driving change and achieving organizational goals. In this chapter, we will explore the significance of effective communication in leadership, examine different communication styles, and provide practical tips for enhancing communication skills.

The Importance of Effective Communication

Effective communication is the cornerstone of successful leadership. It involves conveying ideas clearly, listening actively, and adapting communication styles to connect with diverse audiences. Leaders who communicate effectively inspire trust, build strong relationships, and foster a shared sense of purpose.

"The single biggest problem in communication is the illusion that it has taken place." - George Bernard Shaw

George Bernard Shaw's emphasizes the need for clarity and intentionality in communication. Leaders must ensure that their messages are understood as intended and actively seek feedback to confirm comprehension.

Wangari Maathai, a Kenyan environmental activist and Nobel Laureate, effectively utilized communication to advocate for environmental conservation and women's rights. Through her organization, the Green Belt Movement, she mobilized rural communities to plant trees, restore degraded lands, and empower women. Maathai's ability to communicate her vision and engage diverse stakeholders was instrumental in mobilizing support and bringing attention to environmental issues in Africa.

Moses, a significant biblical figure, demonstrated effective communication skills as he led the Israelites out of slavery in Egypt. Despite initially hesitating due to his self-perceived speech impediment, Moses effectively communicated with Pharaoh, persuading him to release the Israelites. Throughout their journey, Moses communicated God's instructions to the people, leading and guiding them through challenging circumstances. His ability to articulate messages and inspire trust played a pivotal role in his leadership.

Communication Styles: Tailoring the Message

Effective leaders understand that different situations and audiences require different communication styles. They adapt their approach to ensure that their messages resonate with and influence their intended recipients. Some common communication styles include authoritative, collaborative, and motivational. If you are a person who only communicates in one style you might find it difficult to pass your message to audience who don't understand your style.

Nelson Mandela, the renowned South African leader, effectively employed inspirational communication to unite a nation torn apart by apartheid. Through his speeches, Mandela conveyed a message of hope, forgiveness, and reconciliation. His ability to connect emotionally with diverse audiences and inspire them to embrace change played a significant role in the transformation of South Africa.

Practical Tips for Effective Communication

1. **Active Listening:** Leaders should listen attentively, seek to understand, and demonstrate empathy towards others' perspectives.

2. **Clarity and Simplicity:** Messages should be clear, concise, and free from jargon to ensure easy comprehension.

3. **Nonverbal Communication:** Leaders must be mindful of their body language, facial expressions, and gestures, as they can greatly impact how messages are received.

4. **Feedback and Dialogue:** Encouraging open dialogue and seeking feedback fosters a culture of collaboration and continuous improvement.

5. **Emotional Intelligence:** Leaders should be aware of their own emotions and the emotions of others, adapting their communication style to build trust and rapport.

Effective communication is a fundamental skill for 21st-century leaders. By mastering the art of clear and impactful communication, leaders can inspire and influence others, foster collaboration, and drive positive change.

Chapter Nine

LEADING WITH DIVERSITY AND INCLUSION

Leading with Diversity and Inclusion

As a leader in this era, it is essential to embrace diversity and foster inclusion within your organization be it a church, an NGO or a private business organization. The 21st century is marked by a diverse and interconnected global community. By valuing and leveraging the unique perspectives, experiences, and talents of individuals from different backgrounds, leaders can drive innovation, enhance decision-making, and create a culture of belonging. In this chapter, we will explore the importance of diversity and inclusion in leadership, provide strategies for building inclusive organizations, and share real-life stories from Africa that exemplify the transformative power of diversity and inclusion.

The Significance of Diversity and Inclusion

Diversity refers to the representation of different backgrounds, perspectives, and characteristics within a group or organization. Inclusion, on the other hand, involves creating an environment where all individuals feel valued, respected, and have equal opportunities to contribute and succeed. Leaders who prioritize diversity and inclusion harness the full potential of their teams and cultivate a culture of innovation, collaboration, and high performance.

"Diversity is being invited to the party; inclusion is being asked to dance." - Verna Myers

Verna Myers, a renowned diversity advocate, emphasizes the importance of not only embracing diversity but actively including and engaging individuals from diverse backgrounds. Inclusion goes beyond representation and involves creating a sense of belonging and empowerment.

Ibukun Awosika, a Nigerian businesswoman and entrepreneur, exemplifies leadership in promoting diversity and inclusion. As the first female Chairman of First Bank of Nigeria Limited, she has championed gender equality and women's empowerment in the workplace. Awosika actively encourages diversity at all levels of the organization, promotes inclusive practices, and advocates for the development and advancement of women in business. Her leadership demonstrates how embracing diversity and fostering inclusion can drive positive change and success.

Strategies for Building Inclusive Organizations

1. **Cultivate a Culture of Belonging:** Create an environment where all individuals feel welcomed, valued, and respected. Foster a culture that celebrates diversity and encourages open dialogue and collaboration.

2. **Implement Inclusive Hiring Practices:** Promote diversity through unbiased and inclusive recruitment processes. Establish diverse hiring panels, use blind

resume reviews, and actively seek out candidates from underrepresented groups.

3. **Provide Diversity and Inclusion Training:** Offer training programs that raise awareness, educate employees about unconscious biases, and provide tools for creating an inclusive workplace. Encourage ongoing learning and dialogue around diversity and inclusion topics.

4. **Foster Inclusive Leadership:** Develop leaders who embrace diversity, lead by example, and actively promote inclusion. Ensure leaders are accountable for creating and maintaining inclusive practices and behaviors.

5. **Employee Resource Groups:** Establish employee resource groups or affinity networks that provide a platform for employees to connect, share experiences, and advocate for underrepresented groups. These groups can contribute to a sense of belonging and provide valuable insights for organizational growth.

The Mandela Rhodes Scholars Program in South Africa is an example of a transformative initiative that promotes diversity and empowers young leaders. The program awards scholarships to outstanding African students, providing them with educational opportunities and fostering leadership development. By nurturing a diverse community of scholars, the program contributes to social change, cross-cultural understanding, and the advancement of Africa's future leaders.

Promoting Diversity and Inclusion Through Collaboration

1. **Collaborate with Diverse Stakeholders:** Engage with diverse groups, communities, and organizations to foster partnerships, gain different perspectives, and expand networks. Embrace collaboration as a means to drive social impact and innovation.

2. **Sponsorship and Mentorship Programs:** Establish sponsorship and mentorship programs to support individuals from underrepresented groups and provide them with opportunities for growth and advancement. These programs help create a more inclusive leadership pipeline and foster meaningful connections between leaders and emerging talent.

3. **Diversity in Decision-Making:** Ensure diverse perspectives are represented in decision-making processes. Encourage open discussions, seek input from individuals with different backgrounds and experiences, and consider diverse viewpoints when making strategic decisions.

4. **Address Bias and Microaggressions:** Create awareness around unconscious biases and microaggressions that can undermine inclusivity. Provide training and resources to help employees recognize and address biases in themselves and others. Foster a culture

where individuals can speak up about discriminatory behaviors and experiences.

The emergence of tech hubs across Africa illustrates the power of diversity and collaboration in driving innovation and economic growth. These hubs bring together individuals from various backgrounds, including developers, entrepreneurs, and creatives, fostering an environment where diverse perspectives and talents intersect. Through collaboration and shared resources, these tech hubs have been instrumental in propelling Africa's technological advancement and creating opportunities for diverse individuals to thrive in the digital age. Example of such tech hubs is as listed below:

1. **iHub (Nairobi, Kenya):** iHub is one of Africa's most renowned tech hubs and innovation centers. It provides a vibrant space for tech entrepreneurs, developers, and creatives to collaborate, network, and access resources and mentorship. iHub has played a significant role in driving Kenya's tech ecosystem and has incubated successful startups.

2. **CcHUB (Lagos, Nigeria):** CcHUB, also known as the Co-Creation Hub, is a leading tech hub in Nigeria. It offers a platform for startups, innovators, and investors to connect, collaborate, and access support and funding. CcHUB focuses on technology-driven solutions to social

challenges and has been instrumental in nurturing Nigeria's tech ecosystem.

3. **MEST (Accra, Ghana):** MEST (Meltwater Entrepreneurial School of Technology) is an incubator and training program for aspiring entrepreneurs in Africa. It provides a rigorous entrepreneurial training program, access to mentors and resources, and the opportunity to pitch and receive investment. MEST has contributed to the growth of Ghana's startup scene and has expanded its reach to other African countries.

4. **BongoHive (Lusaka, Zambia):** BongoHive is Zambia's first technology and innovation hub. It offers co-working spaces, training programs, and events for startups, tech enthusiasts, and entrepreneurs. BongoHive plays a crucial role in fostering entrepreneurship, providing support, and driving innovation in Zambia.

5. **RLabs (Cape Town, South Africa):** RLabs (Reconstructed Living Labs) is a South African-based social innovation and tech hub. It focuses on empowering marginalized communities through technology, entrepreneurship, and skills development. RLabs provides training, mentorship, and incubation programs to uplift individuals and communities through technology-enabled solutions.

These are just a few examples of the many tech hubs across Africa. Each hub has its unique programs, initiatives, and impact on the local tech ecosystem. They serve as vital platforms for collaboration, knowledge sharing, and the growth of innovative startups in Africa.

Leading with diversity and inclusion in the 21st century is not only a moral imperative but also a strategic advantage. By embracing diversity, fostering inclusion, and actively seeking out different perspectives, leaders can tap into the full potential of their teams, drive innovation, and create a culture of belonging. Real-life stories from Africa highlight the transformative power of diversity and inclusion in driving social change, empowering individuals, and fostering economic growth. As leaders, it is our responsibility to champion diversity, create inclusive environments, and collaborate across diverse networks to shape a brighter and more inclusive future. By doing so, we can navigate the complexities of the 21st century and lead with purpose, impact, and integrity.

Chapter Ten

LEADING THROUGH CHANGE AND UNCERTAINTY

Leading Through Change and Uncertainty

As leaders, we are tasked with navigating through these turbulent waters and guiding our teams with clarity and resilience. In the 21st century, change and uncertainty have become constants in our personal and professional lives. This chapter explores the essential qualities and strategies for leading through change and uncertainty, helping leaders embrace the challenges, inspire their teams, and drive positive outcomes in an ever-evolving world.

The Nature of Change and Uncertainty

Change and uncertainty can manifest in various forms, including technological advancements, economic fluctuations, shifting market dynamics, and unexpected events like pandemics or geopolitical shifts. Leaders must recognize that change is inevitable and approach uncertainty as an opportunity for growth and adaptation.

"Change is the only constant in life." - Heraclitus

Heraclitus, an ancient Greek philosopher, recognized the perpetual nature of change. As leaders, we must embrace this reality and cultivate the skills to effectively lead through change and uncertainty.

The Role of the 21st Century Leader

In an era marked by rapid change and uncertainty, the role of a leader goes beyond traditional command and control. A 21st century leader must exhibit the following qualities:

1. **Adaptability:** Leaders need to be flexible and open-minded, embracing change as an opportunity for innovation and growth. They must adapt their strategies, approaches, and mindsets to meet evolving circumstances.

2. **Vision and Strategic Thinking:** Leaders must have a clear vision of the future and communicate it effectively to inspire and align their teams. They should engage in strategic thinking, anticipating trends, and proactively shaping the direction of their organizations.

3. **Resilience and Emotional Intelligence:** Leading through change and uncertainty requires emotional intelligence and resilience. Leaders must manage their emotions, demonstrate empathy, and provide support to their teams during challenging times.

The story of Nokia, once the world's leading mobile phone manufacturer, serves as a powerful example of both the impact of change and the need for adaptive leadership. Nokia initially dominated the mobile phone market but failed to anticipate and adapt to the rise of smartphones. The company's failure to embrace the changing landscape led to a decline in market share. However, Nokia's subsequent transformation under new leadership demonstrates the power of adaptability. The company shifted its focus to telecommunications infrastructure and emerged as a key player in the 5G network market. Nokia's journey highlights the importance of visionary leadership and adaptability in the face of change.

Strategies for Leading Through Change and Uncertainty

1. **Communicate Transparently:** Effective communication is crucial during times of change and uncertainty. Leaders should provide clear and timely information, share the rationale behind decisions, and address concerns openly. Transparency builds trust and helps employees navigate uncertainty with confidence.

2. **Foster a Growth Mindset:** Encourage a growth mindset within the organization, promoting a culture of continuous learning and adaptation. Emphasize that challenges and setbacks are opportunities for growth and improvement, encouraging employees to embrace change rather than fear it.

3. **Empower and Involve Employees:** In times of change, involve employees in decision-making processes, seeking their input and feedback. Empower them to take

ownership of their work, fostering a sense of ownership and commitment.

4. **Lead by Example:** As a leader, model the behavior you expect from your team. Demonstrate resilience, adaptability, and a positive attitude towards change. Your actions and attitude will set the tone for how others perceive and respond to change.

5. **Provide Support and Resources:** During times of uncertainty, provide the necessary support, resources, and training to help employees navigate change successfully. Offer coaching, mentorship, and development opportunities to build their capacity to adapt and thrive.

As leaders, we must embrace change as an opportunity for growth and innovation. By communicating transparently, fostering a growth mindset, empowering employees, leading by example, and providing support, we can guide our teams through uncertain times and inspire them to achieve remarkable outcomes.

Remember, leading through change and uncertainty is not just about surviving; it's about thriving and creating a better future for ourselves, our organizations, and the communities we serve. As leaders in the 21st century, we have the opportunity and responsibility to shape a positive and resilient future through our adaptive leadership.

Chapter Eleven

LEADING REMOTE AND VIRTUAL TEAMS

Leading Remote and Virtual Teams

The rise of technology and the changing nature of work have given rise to remote and virtual teams. Leading teams that are geographically dispersed presents unique challenges and opportunities for leaders. This chapter explores the key principles and strategies for effectively leading remote and virtual teams, ensuring collaboration, productivity, and engagement across distances.

The Rise of Remote and Virtual Teams

Advancements in communication technology, globalization, and the evolving nature of work have contributed to the increasing prevalence of remote and virtual teams. These teams consist of individuals who work together from different locations, leveraging technology to communicate, collaborate, and achieve shared goals.

"The strength of the team is each individual member. The strength of each member is the team." - Phil Jackson

Phil Jackson, a renowned basketball coach, emphasizes the importance of teamwork in achieving success. This principle holds true for remote and virtual teams, where individuals must work collaboratively despite physical separation.

Key Principles for Leading Remote and Virtual Teams

1. **Clear Communication:** Effective communication is essential when leading remote and virtual teams. Establish clear channels for communication, set expectations regarding response times, and encourage regular check-ins to ensure everyone is aligned and informed.

2. **Building Trust:** Trust is the foundation of successful remote teamwork. Foster trust by demonstrating transparency, accountability, and reliability. Encourage open and honest communication, provide feedback, and celebrate achievements to build a sense of trust and camaraderie.

3. **Goal Alignment:** Ensure that team members understand the team's goals and how their individual contributions align with the overall objectives. Clearly define expectations, deliverables, and timelines to promote clarity and focus.

Andela, a tech company founded in Nigeria, provides a real-life example of successfully leading remote and virtual teams. With a distributed engineering workforce across Africa, Andela leverages technology and effective leadership practices to manage remote teams. They emphasize clear communication, goal alignment, and continuous learning to foster a culture of collaboration and productivity. Andela's success demonstrates that remote and virtual teams can thrive when supported by effective leadership practices.

Strategies for Leading Remote and Virtual Teams

1. **Utilize Technology:** Leverage technology tools that facilitate seamless communication and collaboration. Platforms such as video conferencing, project management software, and instant messaging enable team members to connect and work together regardless of physical distance.

2. **Foster Team Bonding:** Create opportunities for team members to build relationships and develop rapport. Encourage virtual team-building activities, such as online games, virtual coffee breaks, or sharing personal stories, to foster a sense of camaraderie and connection.

3. **Set Clear Expectations:** Clearly define roles, responsibilities, and performance expectations. Establish guidelines for availability, response times, and virtual meeting etiquette to ensure everyone is on the same page.

4. **Encourage Autonomy and Empowerment:** Trust your remote team members to make decisions and take ownership of their work. Provide autonomy, support their professional development, and empower them to make independent decisions, fostering a sense of ownership and accountability.

GitLab, a tech company specializing in software development, operates with a remote-first approach, where employees work remotely by default. By embracing remote work, GitLab has fostered a culture of autonomy, flexibility, and collaboration. They utilize technology, transparent communication practices, and clear documentation to enable effective remote teamwork. GitLab's example demonstrates the possibilities and benefits of remote-first approaches when supported by strong leadership practices.

Leading remote and virtual teams requires a unique set of skills and strategies to overcome geographical barriers and ensure successful collaboration. By prioritizing clear communication, building trust, and aligning goals, leaders can effectively lead remote teams and virtual teams in the 21st century. Real-life examples, such as Andela's distributed engineering teams and GitLab's remote-first approach, illustrate the power of effective leadership practices in supporting remote work and achieving team success.

Leaders must utilize technology tools to enable seamless communication and collaboration among remote team members. Platforms like video conferencing, project management software, and instant messaging foster connectivity and facilitate effective teamwork. By leveraging these tools, leaders can bridge the gap created by physical distance and promote engagement and productivity.

Fostering team bonding is crucial for remote and virtual teams. Leaders should create opportunities for team members to interact, share experiences, and build relationships. Virtual team-building activities, regular check-ins, and moments of informal connection help foster a sense of belonging and camaraderie, despite the physical separation.

Setting clear expectations is paramount in leading remote teams. Clearly defining roles, responsibilities, and performance expectations ensures that everyone understands their contributions and responsibilities. Establishing guidelines for availability, response times, and virtual meeting etiquette helps maintain accountability and cohesion within the team.

Chapter Twelve

NURTURING CREATIVITY AND INNOVATION

Nurturing Creativity and Innovation

In the fast-paced and ever-changing landscape of the 21st century, organizations must prioritize creativity and innovation to stay competitive and adapt to new challenges. As a leader, nurturing a culture of creativity and fostering innovation within your team is crucial. This chapter explores strategies for nurturing creativity, promoting innovation, and creating an environment that supports and encourages new ideas.

The Importance of Creativity and Innovation

"Creativity is intelligence having fun." - Albert Einstein

Albert Einstein's captures the essence of creativity as a dynamic and joyful expression of intelligence. Creativity drives innovation, enabling organizations to find new solutions, seize opportunities, and differentiate themselves in the marketplace. In the 21st century, where disruption is constant, fostering creativity and nurturing innovation are essential for sustained success.

Creating an Environment for Creativity

1. **Embrace a Growth Mindset:** Foster a culture that embraces learning, experimentation, and risk-taking. Encourage team members to see failures as learning opportunities and to continually seek new knowledge and skills.

2. **Encourage Diverse Perspectives:** Embrace diversity of thought and encourage team members to bring their unique perspectives to the table. Create opportunities for collaboration, brainstorming, and idea-sharing to leverage the collective intelligence of the team.

3. **Provide Psychological Safety:** Create an environment where team members feel safe to express their ideas, ask questions, and challenge the status quo. Encourage open and respectful communication, and create forums for constructive feedback and dialogue.

The story of M-Pesa, a mobile money transfer service in Kenya, showcases the power of innovation in transforming lives. By leveraging the widespread adoption of mobile phones, M-Pesa revolutionized financial services, allowing people to send and receive money securely and conveniently. M-Pesa's success stemmed from the creativity and entrepreneurial spirit of its founders, who saw an opportunity to address a pressing need in their community. This real-life example demonstrates how innovation can lead to significant positive impact.

Promoting Innovation

1. **Foster a Culture of Curiosity:** Encourage curiosity and a thirst for knowledge among team members. Encourage them to explore new ideas, ask questions, and challenge existing processes or assumptions. Provide

resources and support for continuous learning and professional development.

2. **Provide Resources for Innovation:** Allocate dedicated time, budget, and resources for innovation projects. Create innovation labs or designated spaces where team members can experiment, collaborate, and develop new ideas without the fear of failure.

3. **Support Risk-Taking:** Encourage calculated risk-taking and provide support when team members propose innovative ideas. Celebrate both successes and failures as opportunities for growth and learning.

4. **Recognize and Reward Innovation:** Acknowledge and reward innovative thinking and achievements within the team. This can include public recognition, incentives, or opportunities for career advancement for those who contribute to the organization's innovation initiatives.

Safaricom, a leading telecommunications company in Kenya, established an innovation center in Nairobi to foster creativity and innovation. The center provides a collaborative space where employees and external stakeholders can experiment, co-create, and develop innovative solutions. Safaricom's commitment to innovation has resulted in the development of groundbreaking services and products such as the M-Pesa earlier mentioned, solidifying its position as a market leader.

In the rapidly evolving landscape of the 21st century, nurturing creativity and fostering innovation is vital for organizations to stay relevant and competitive. By creating an environment that embraces a growth mindset, encourages diverse perspectives, provides psychological safety, and supports risk-taking, leaders can cultivate a culture of creativity and innovation within their teams. Real-life stories, such as the innovation of M-Pesa and Safaricom's innovation center in Nairobi, highlight the transformative power of creativity and innovation.

As leaders, we must prioritize the nurturing of creativity and innovation by creating an environment that supports and encourages new ideas. Embracing a growth mindset and fostering a culture of learning and experimentation allows team members to explore their creative potential and take calculated risks. By encouraging diverse perspectives and providing psychological safety, we create a space where individuals feel empowered to share their ideas and challenge the status quo.

Providing resources and support for innovation is crucial. Allocating dedicated time, budget, and physical spaces for innovation projects allows team members to focus on developing new ideas and solutions. Supporting risk-taking and recognizing both successes and failures as opportunities for growth and learning further encourages an innovative mindset.

Real-life stories, such as the innovation of M-Pesa and Safaricom's innovation center, demonstrate the impact that creativity and innovation can have on individuals, organizations, and even entire communities. These examples inspire us to think outside the box, push boundaries, and embrace the possibilities of innovation.

In conclusion, nurturing creativity and fostering innovation is a critical responsibility for leaders in the 21st century. By creating an environment that values and encourages new ideas, supporting risk-taking, and providing resources for innovation, leaders can unlock the creative potential of their teams and drive innovation forward. Embracing creativity and innovation allows organizations to adapt, grow, and thrive in an ever-changing world. Let us embrace the power of creativity and innovation as catalysts for success in the 21st century.

Chapter Thirteen

SUSTAINING PERSONAL WELL-BEING AS A LEADER

Sustaining Personal Well-being as a Leader

In the fast-paced and demanding world of leadership, it is essential to prioritize personal well-being. The 21st-century leader faces numerous challenges and responsibilities that can take a toll on their physical, mental, and emotional health. This chapter explores strategies for sustaining personal well-being as a leader, ensuring a healthy work-life balance, managing stress, and prioritizing self-care.

The Importance of Personal Well-being

As a leader, your well-being directly impacts your ability to lead effectively. Taking care of yourself allows you to maintain focus, make better decisions, and inspire and motivate your team. It sets an example for others and fosters a positive work culture that values well-being.

"It is not selfish to love yourself, take care of yourself, and to make your happiness a priority. It's necessary."
- Mandy Hale

Mandy Hale's emphasizes the importance of prioritizing self-care and well-being. As leaders, we must recognize that taking care of ourselves is not selfish but necessary for our personal and professional success.

Maintaining Work-Life Balance

1. **Set Boundaries:** Establish clear boundaries between work and personal life. Define specific working hours and communicate them to your team. Avoid excessive work hours and learn to disconnect from work during personal time.

2. **Delegate and Empower:** Delegate tasks to your team members, allowing them to take ownership and develop their skills. Empowering others not only lightens your workload but also promotes a sense of trust and growth within the team.

Joshua Selman Nimmak, a renowned Nigerian preacher, teacher, and conference speaker known for his powerful teachings and impactful ministry. Despite the demands of his ministry and the constant travel and speaking engagements, Joshua Selman understands the importance of sustaining his personal well-being.

After completing series of intense speaking tour, where he delivered back-to-back sermons and teachings in different cities across the country pouring out his heart and soul, ministering to thousands of people. He still realizes that he needs to take some time for himself, to rejuvenate and replenish his own spiritual, physical, and emotional reserves.

He makes it a conscious thing to retreat to a serene and secluded location, away from the hustle and bustle of ministry life. Joshua Selman finds solace in the quietness of nature, where he can connect with God and recharge his spiritual batteries. Surrounded by the beauty of creation, he spends hours in prayer, meditation, and study of the Scriptures, seeking divine guidance and renewal.

Joshua Selman also recognized the importance of physical well-being in sustaining his ministry. He makes it a point to prioritize exercise and eat healthily. He engages in regular physical activities to keep his body fit and energized. He understands that taking care of his physical health will enhance his overall well-being and enable him to continue serving others effectively.

Furthermore, Joshua Selman Nimmak understands the power of relationships and community in sustaining personal well-being. He surrounds himself with a supportive network of family, friends, and fellow believers who provide encouragement, counsel, and accountability. He values quality time spent with love ones, enjoying moments of laughter, deep conversations, and shared experiences.

In addition to taking care of his spiritual and physical well-being, Joshua Selman also pursues his hobbies and interests that bring him joy and relaxation. He enjoys reading books outside the realm of ministry and listening to uplifting music. Engaging in these activities allows him to tap into his creativity and find balance in his life.

Joshua Selman's commitment to sustaining his personal well-being not only benefits him but also enhances his ministry. By taking time to nurture his own spiritual, physical, and emotional health, he is better equipped to minister to others with authenticity, compassion, and wisdom.

His lifestyle should serve as a reminder to leaders that prioritizing personal well-being is essential for long-term success and impact. Just as Joshua Selman finds time to retreat, connect with God, take care of his physical health, and engage in activities that bring him joy, leaders should also carve out moments for self-care and create a healthy work-life balance. By sustaining personal well-being, leaders can continue to serve, inspire, and make a difference in the lives of others.

Managing Stress and Building Resilience

1. **Practice Mindfulness:** Incorporate mindfulness techniques, such as meditation, deep breathing exercises, or journaling, into your daily routine. These practices help reduce stress, increase self-awareness, and promote overall well-being.

2. **Seek Support:** Surround yourself with a supportive network of colleagues, mentors, or friends who can provide guidance, encouragement, and a listening ear. Sharing your challenges and seeking advice can help alleviate stress and provide fresh perspectives. Seeking

help is not a sign of weakness rather it shows strength as a leader.

3. **Build Resilience:** Develop resilience by embracing challenges as learning opportunities, focusing on solutions rather than problems, and cultivating a positive mindset. Resilience allows you to bounce back from setbacks and maintain a strong sense of well-being.

Oprah Winfrey, a media mogul and philanthropist, has faced numerous challenges throughout her career. From childhood trauma to professional setbacks, she has demonstrated remarkable resilience. Through self-reflection, therapy, and a commitment to personal growth, Oprah has overcome adversity and maintained her well-being while continuing to inspire others.

Prioritizing Self-Care

1. **Practice Self-Compassion:** Be kind to yourself and treat yourself with the same compassion and understanding you would extend to others. Embrace self-care activities that bring you joy and relaxation.

2. **Physical Well-being:** Prioritize exercise, healthy eating, and sufficient sleep. Regular physical activity, a balanced diet, and adequate rest are essential for maintaining energy levels, reducing stress, and promoting overall well-being.

3. **Pursue Hobbies and Interests**: Engage in activities outside of work that bring you fulfillment and joy. Pursuing hobbies and interests allows you to recharge, tap into your creativity, and find balance in your life.

Sustaining personal well-being is crucial for leaders in the 21st century. By prioritizing work-life balance, managing stress, and prioritizing self-care, leaders can ensure their physical, mental, and emotional well-being. Real-life stories of leaders like Joshua Selman remind us of the importance of self-care in maintaining resilience, making a positive impact, and inspiring others.

As leaders, we must recognize that our well-being is not a luxury but a necessity. Taking care of ourselves allows us to lead effectively, maintain balance, and set an example for others. By embracing personal well-being, we create a foundation for sustainable success and fulfillment in our leadership journey. Let us prioritize self-care and well-being, not just for ourselves but for the betterment of our teams and the organizations we lead.

Final Note

As we conclude this book, I hope that the insights, stories, and practical advice shared within its pages have inspired and empowered you to embrace your leadership potential. May you be a leader who makes a positive impact, shapes the future, and leaves a lasting legacy in the 21st century and beyond.

Remember, leadership is not just about achieving personal success, but about empowering others, fostering collaboration, and making a difference in the world. It is a continuous journey of growth, learning, and self-discovery. Embrace the challenges, embrace the opportunities, and embrace the role of a 21st-century leader.

Thank you for joining us on this enlightening exploration of leadership in the 21st century. May you lead with courage, integrity, and a vision that inspires others to reach their full potential.

About the Author

Karngong Lovett Tangwa is a dynamic and multifaceted individual with a passion for technology, leadership, and personal development. He holds a Bachelor's degree in Computer Engineering from the esteemed Federal University of Technology Minna, where he honed his skills and knowledge in the realm of technology.

As a cyber security enthusiast, Karngong has always been fascinated by the ever-evolving world of digital security. He actively seeks to stay updated with the latest trends and developments in the field, driven by a strong desire to contribute to a safer and more secure cyberspace.

Beyond his technical prowess, Karngong is a devoted advocate for leadership excellence. He firmly believes that great leaders are not born but are cultivated through continuous learning, adaptability, and a commitment to serving others. With a vision of nurturing a new generation of leaders, Karngong strives to inspire and empower individuals to discover and harness their leadership potential.

In addition to his advocacy for leadership, Karngong is a talented and prolific writer. He has authored several